Ebony Girls

HOT SEXY EBONY LINGERIE GIRLS MODELS PICTURES

By **EROTICA PHOTO ART LOVER**

Copyright © Ebony Girls

ALL RIGHTS RESERVED. NO PART OF THIS DOCUMENT MAY BE REPRODUCED OR TRANSMITTED IN ANY FORM OR BY ANY MEANS, ELECTRONIC, MECHANICAL, PHOTOCOPYING, RECORDING, OR OTHERWISE, WITHOUT PRIOR WRITTEN PERMISSION OF EROTICA PHOTO ART LOVER.

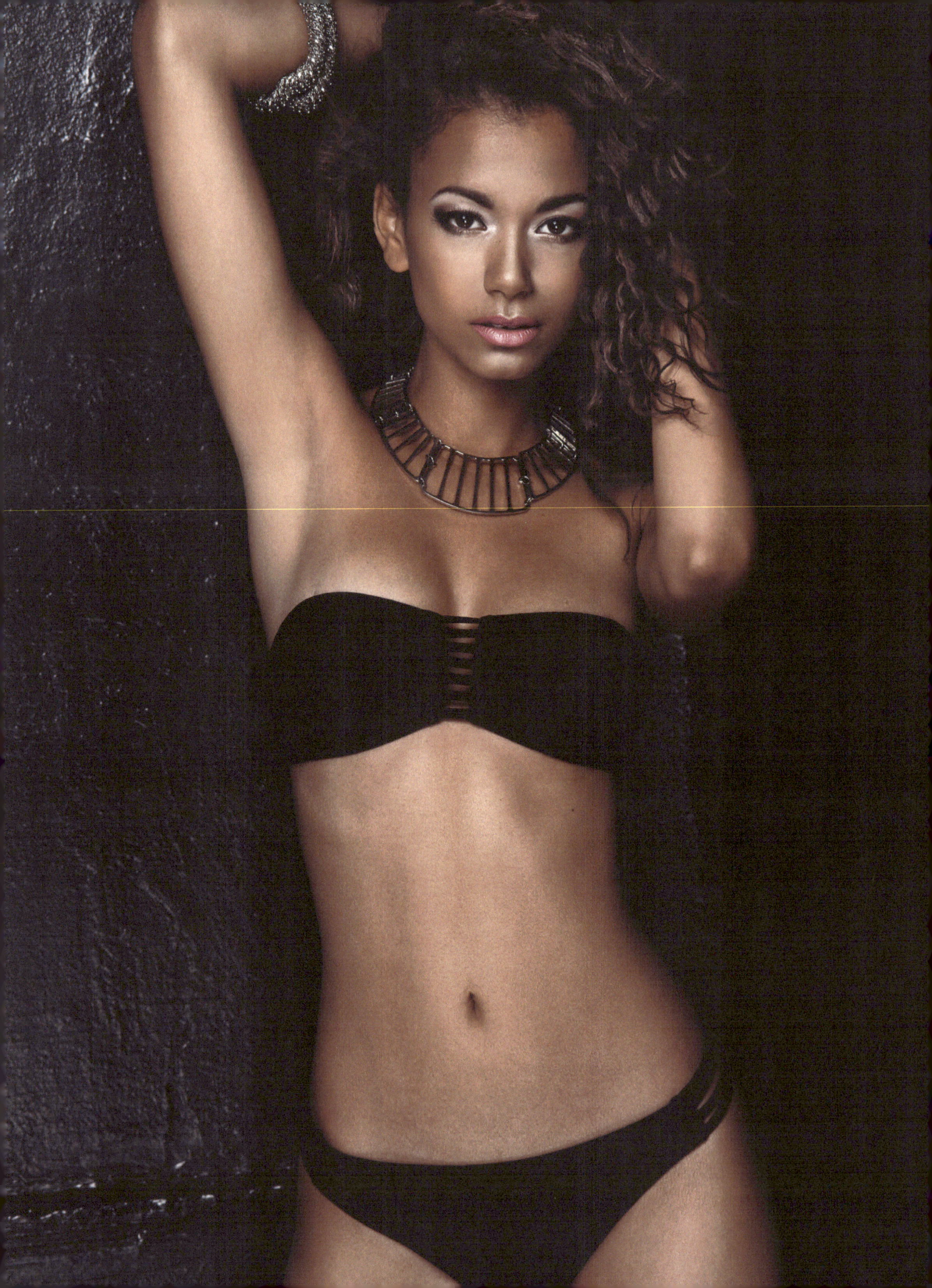

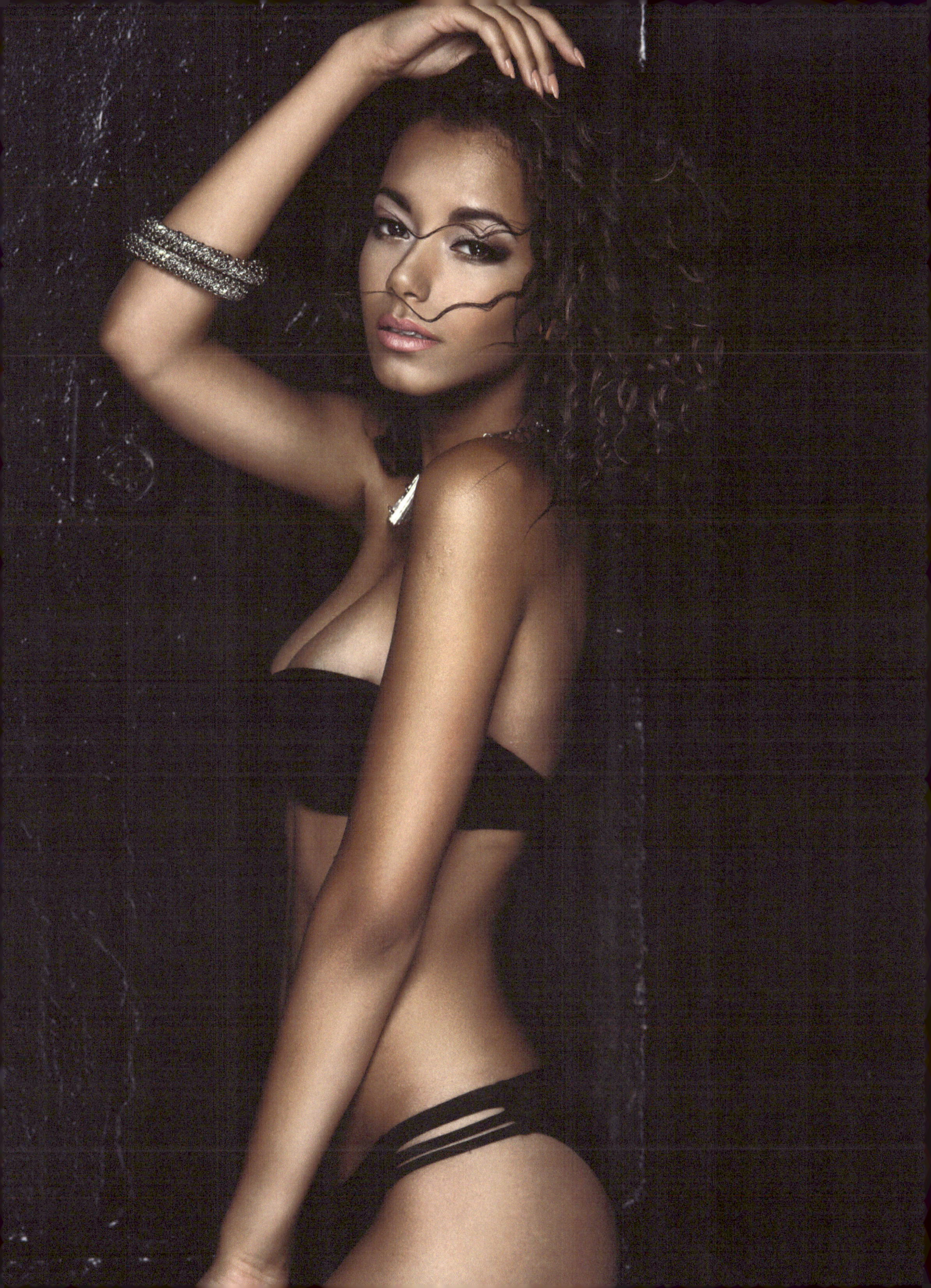

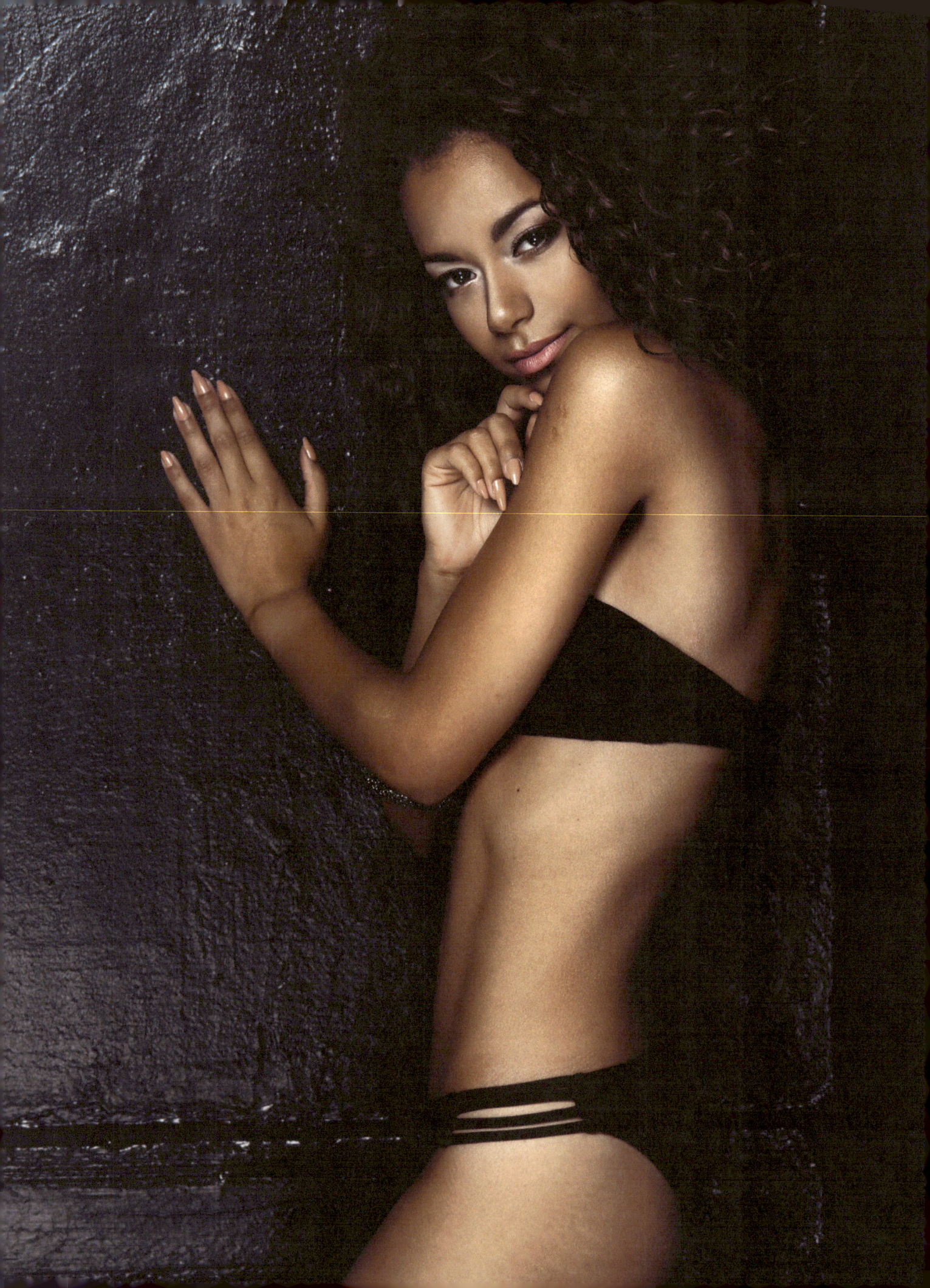

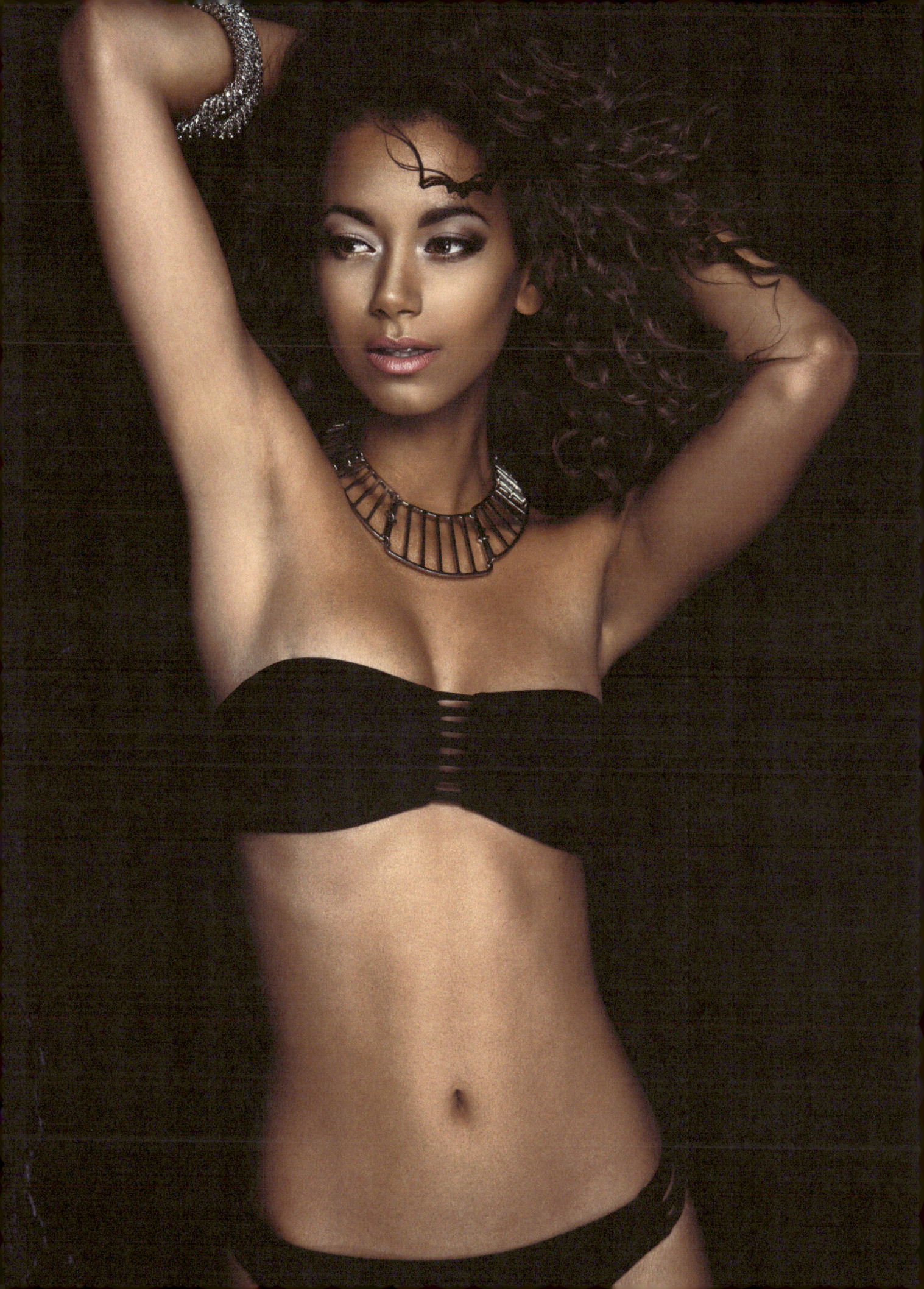

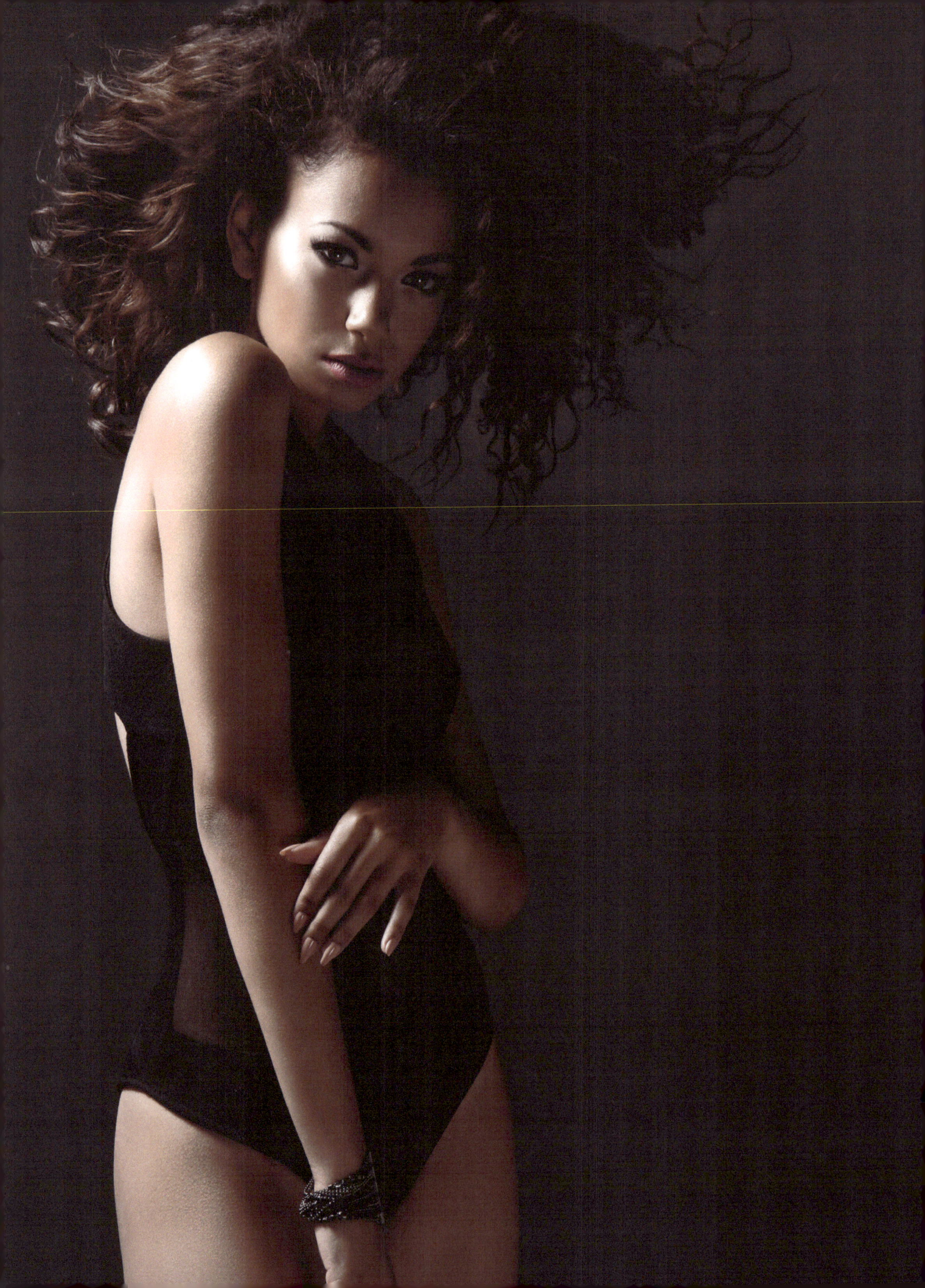

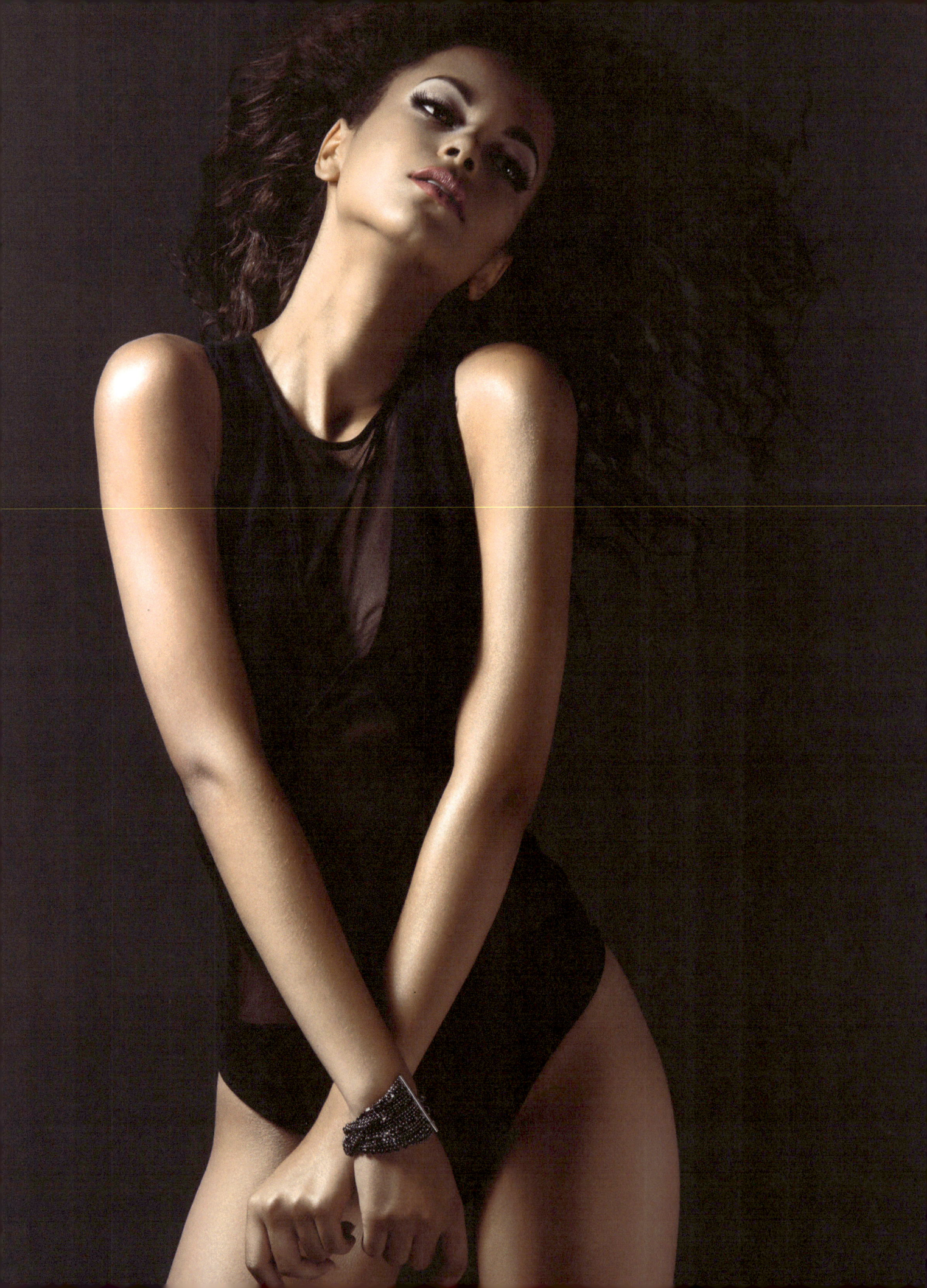

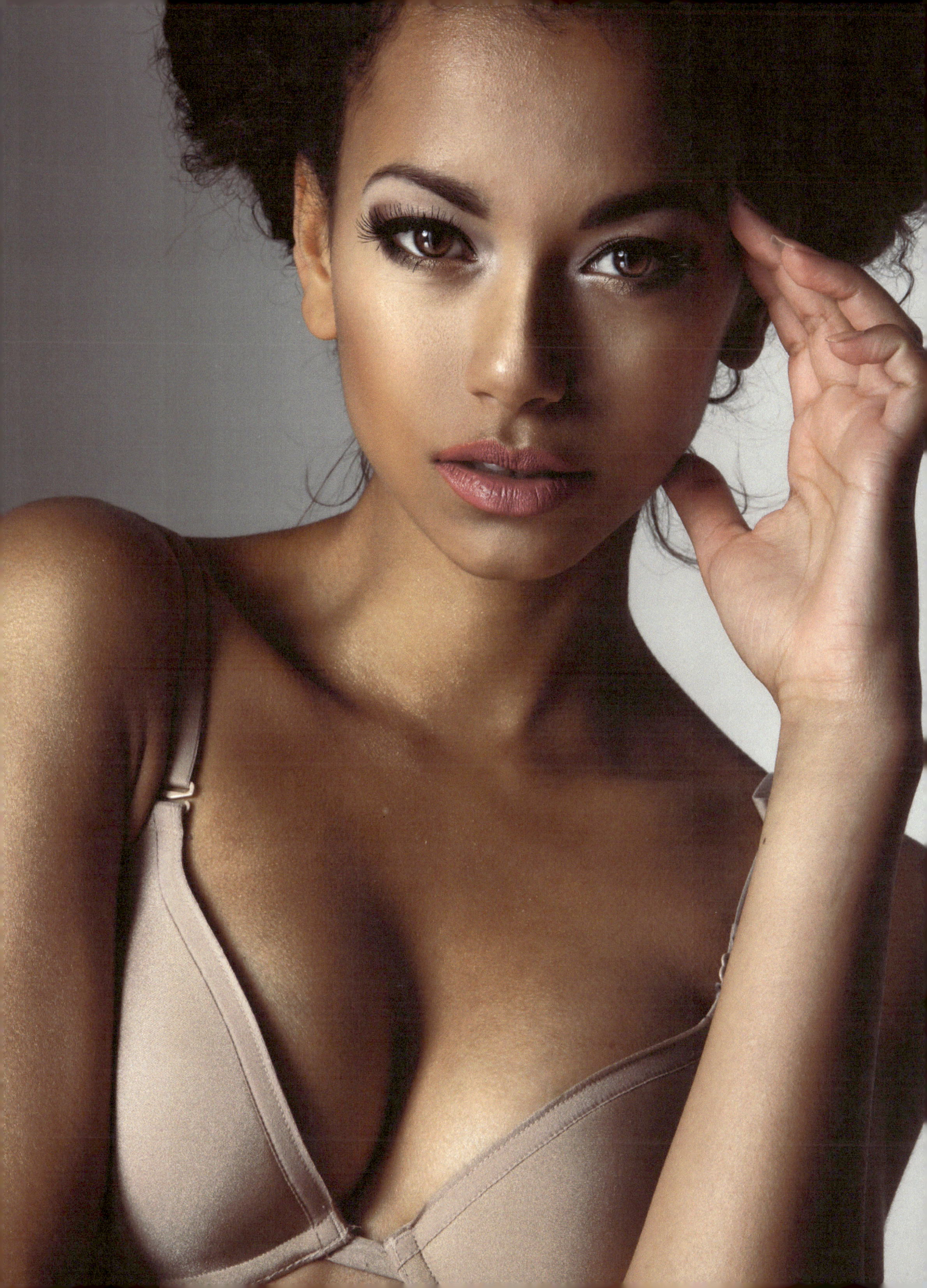

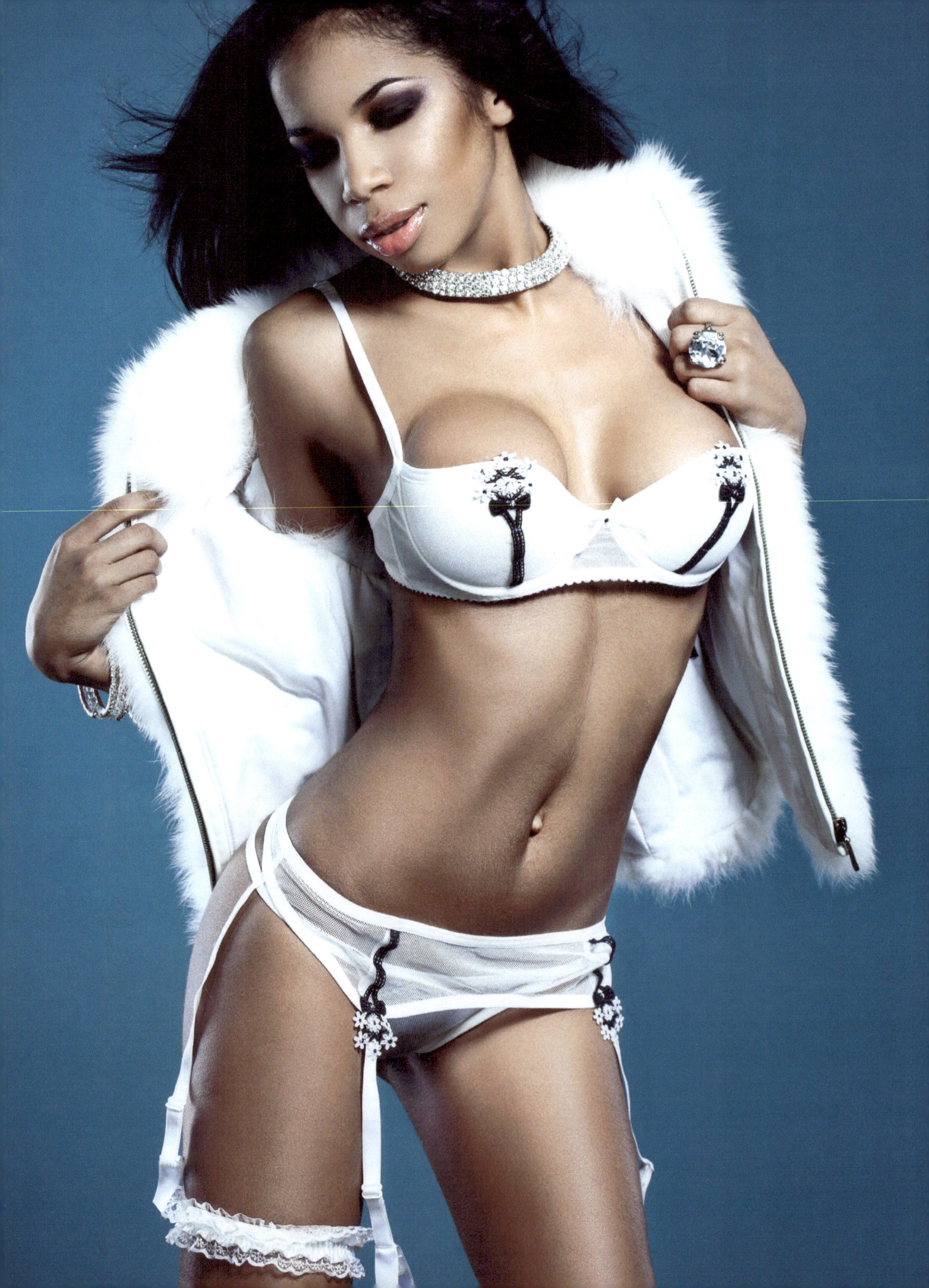

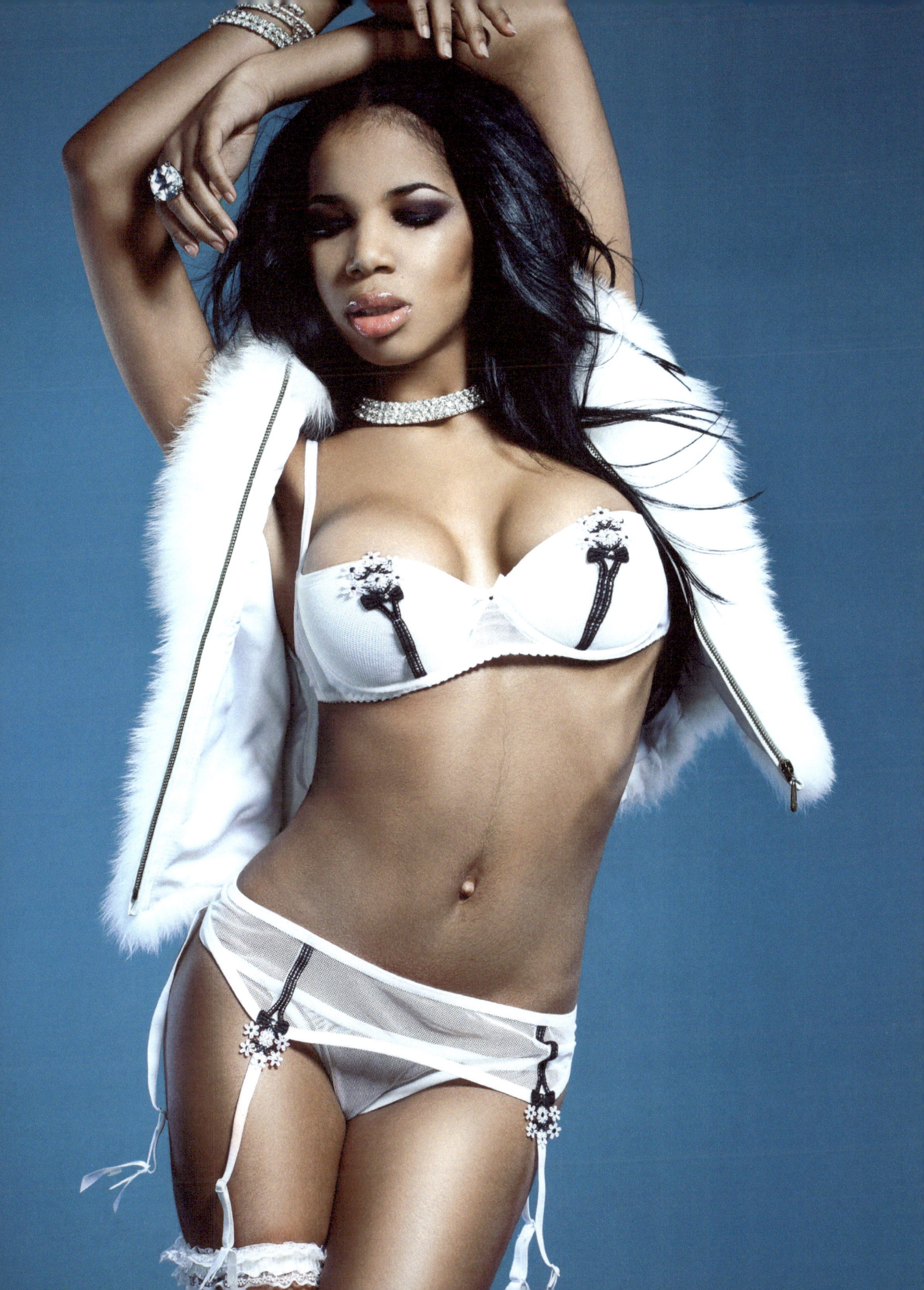

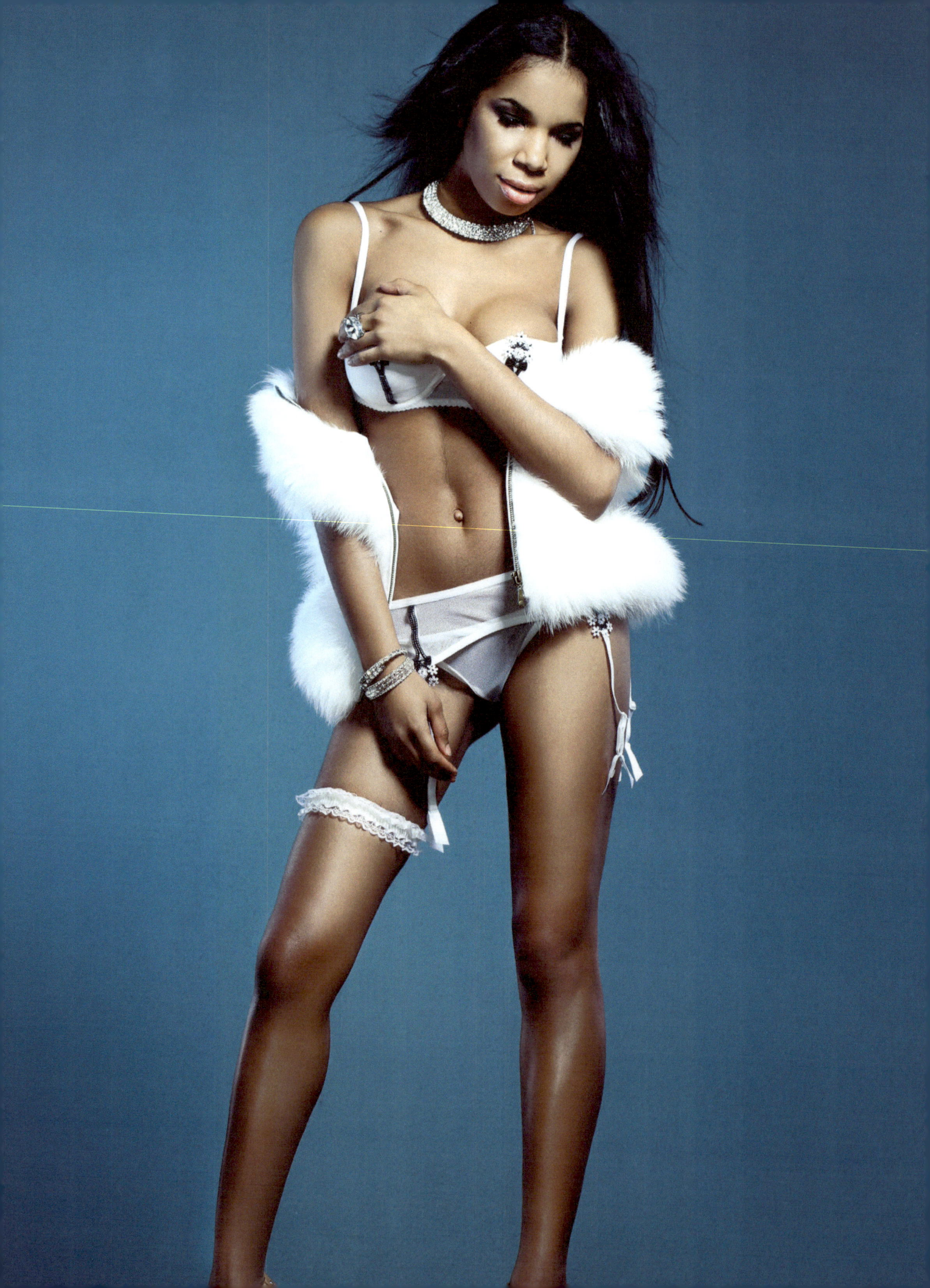

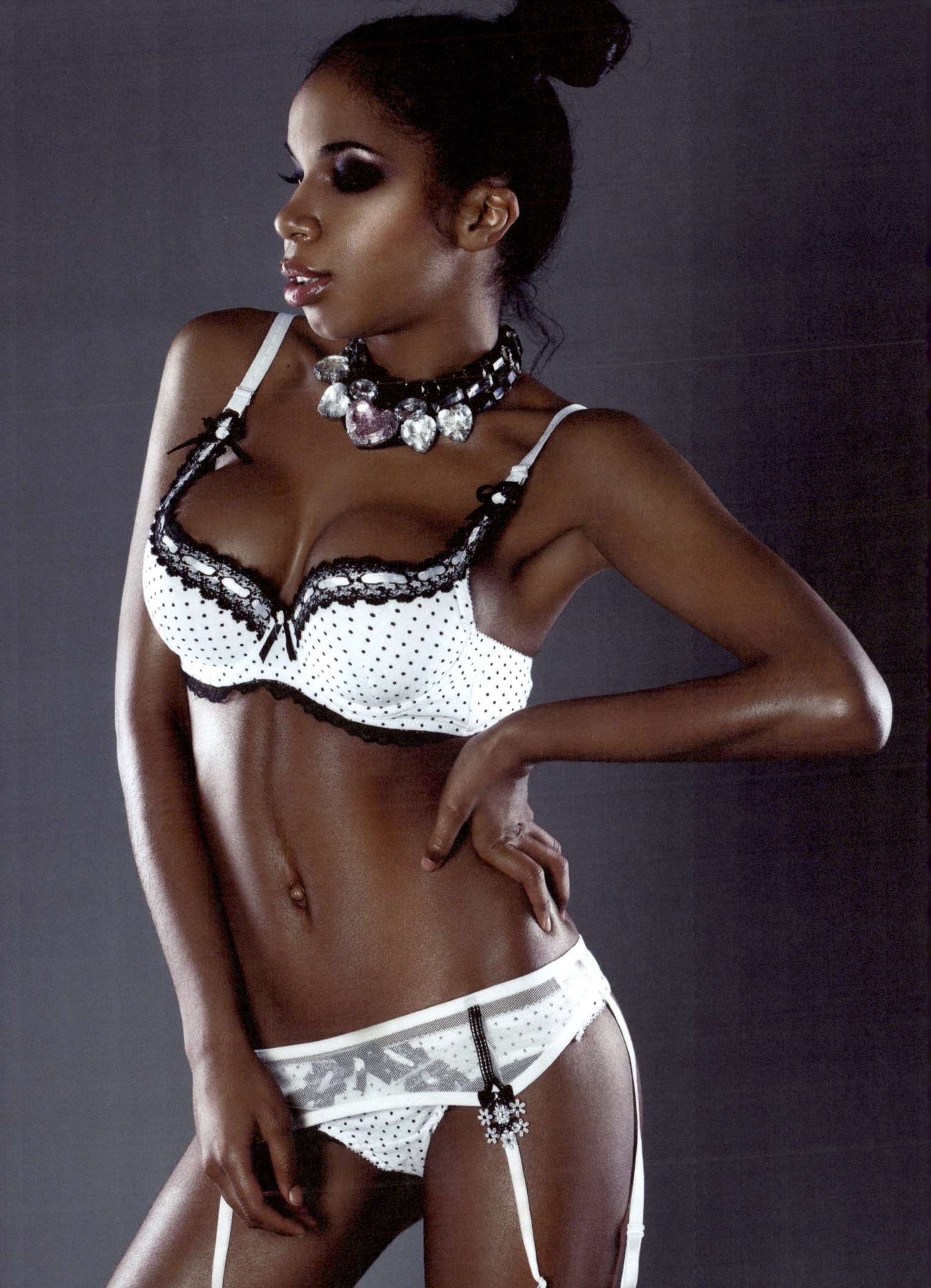

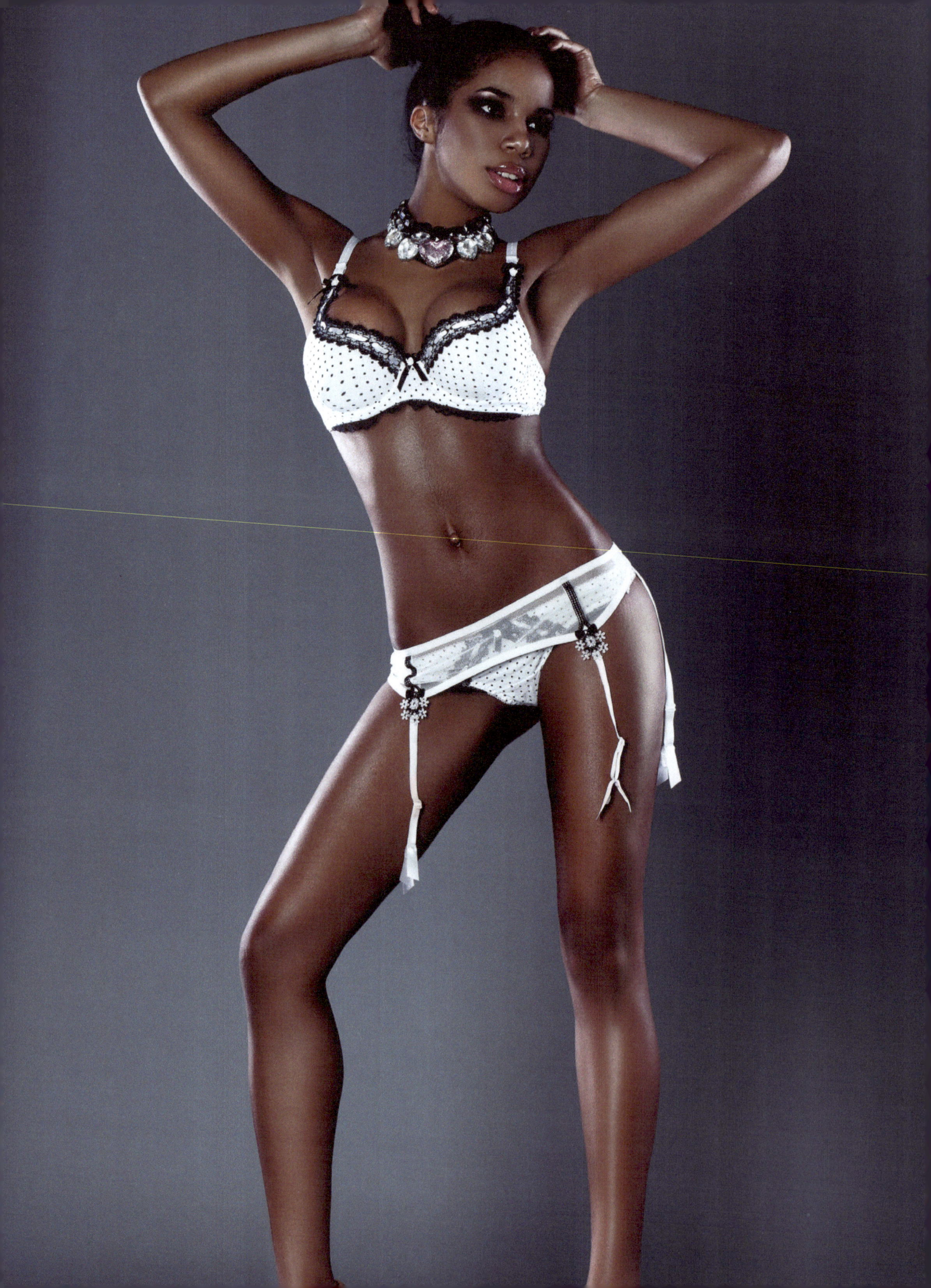

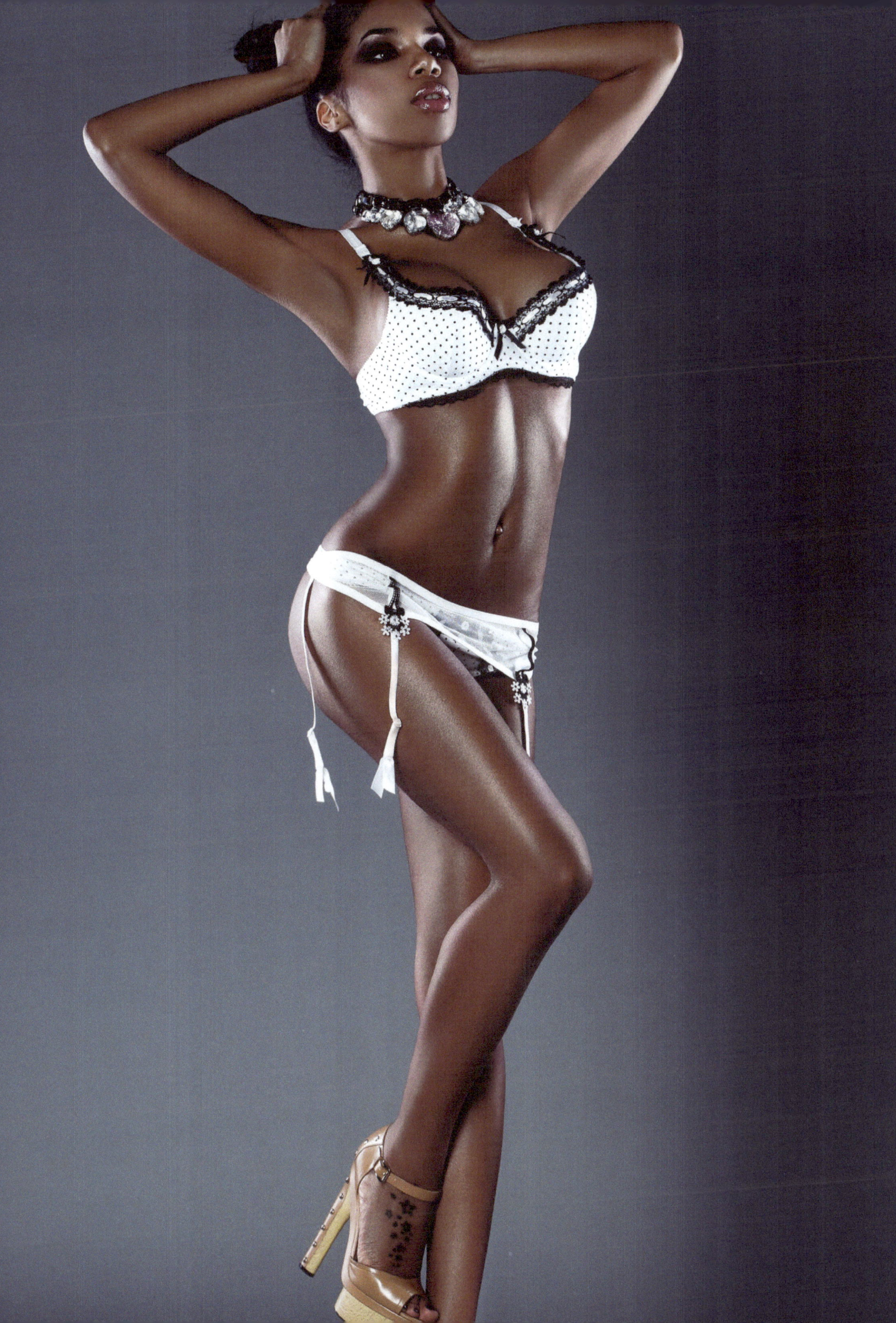

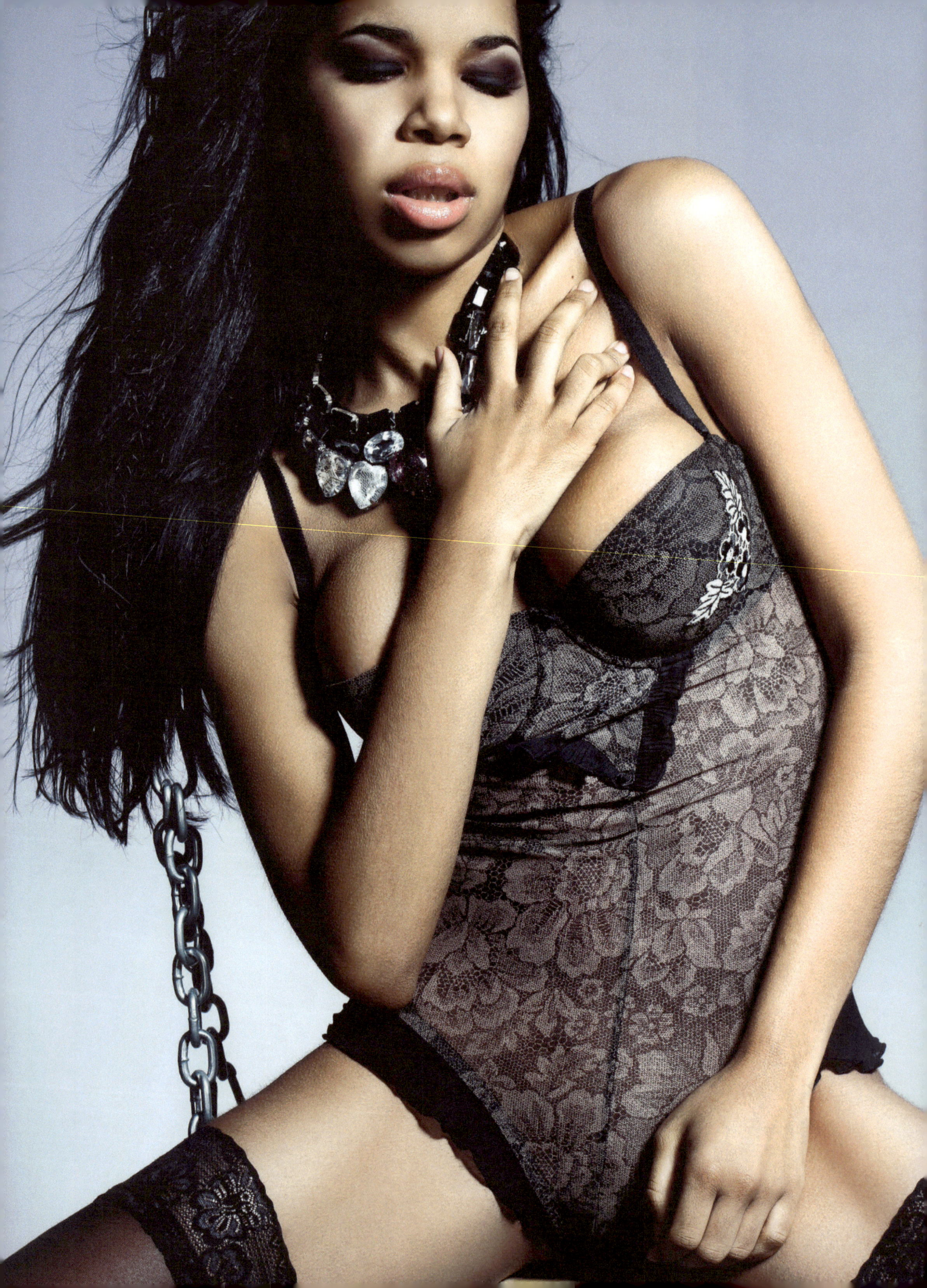

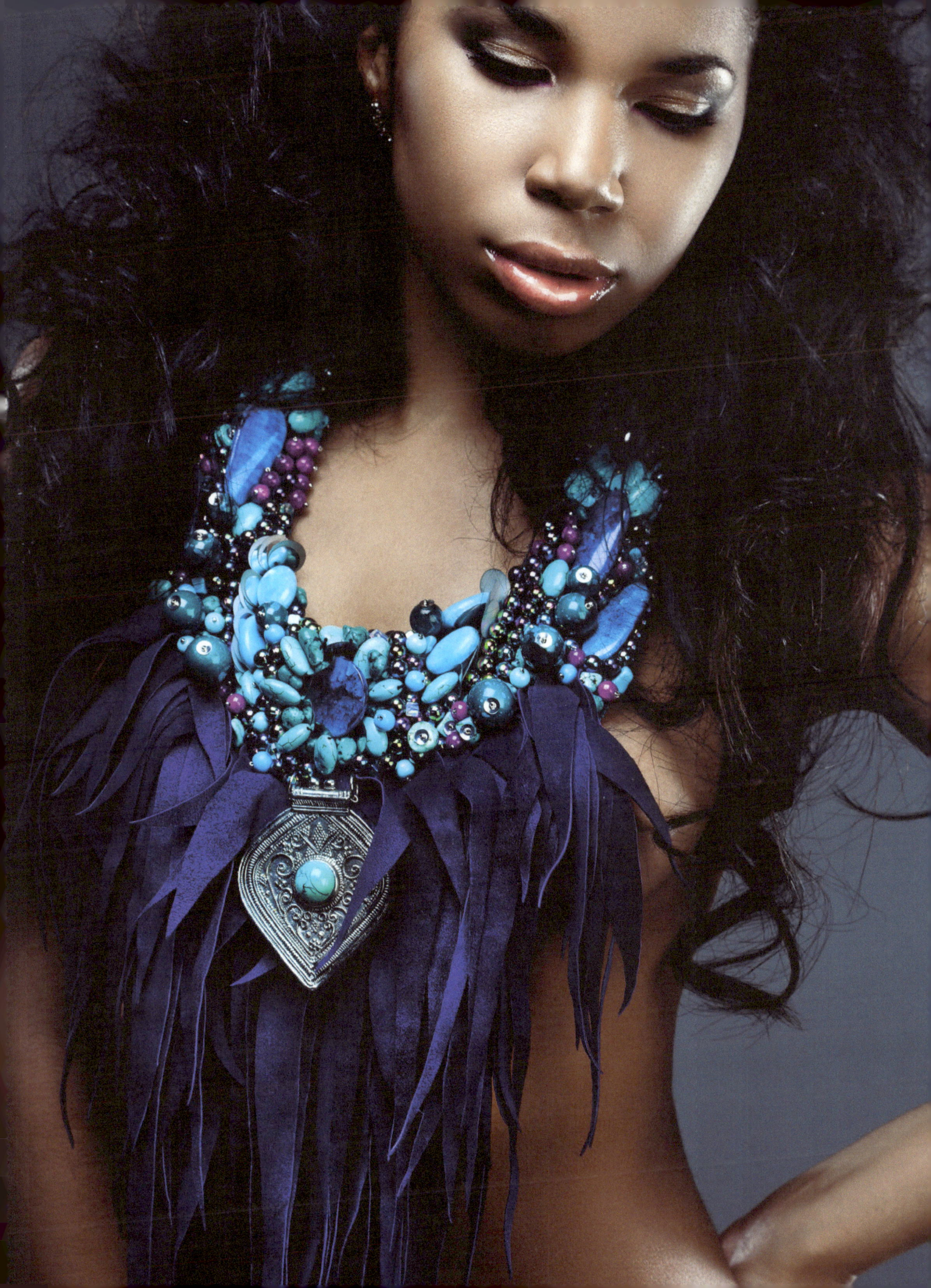

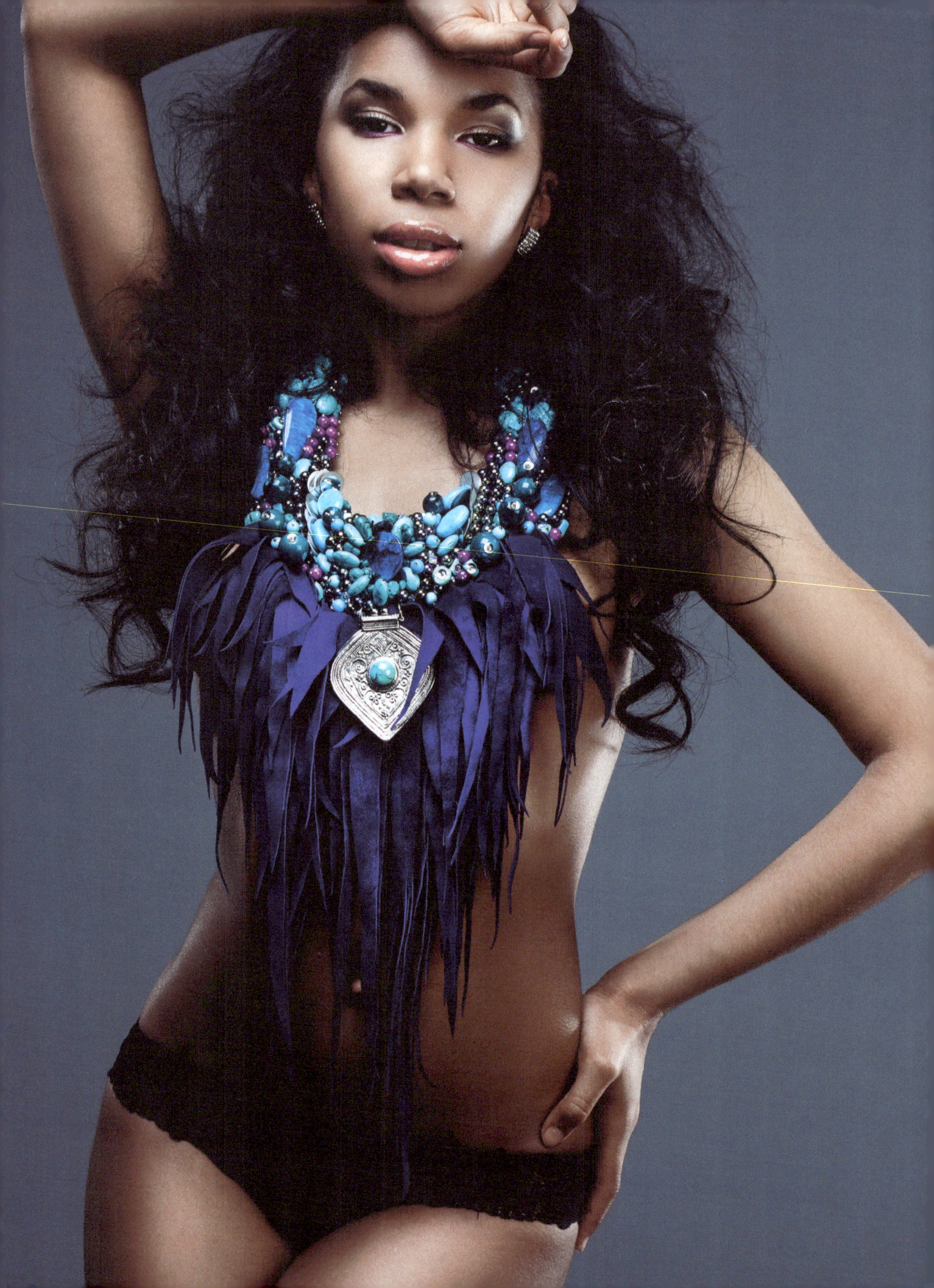

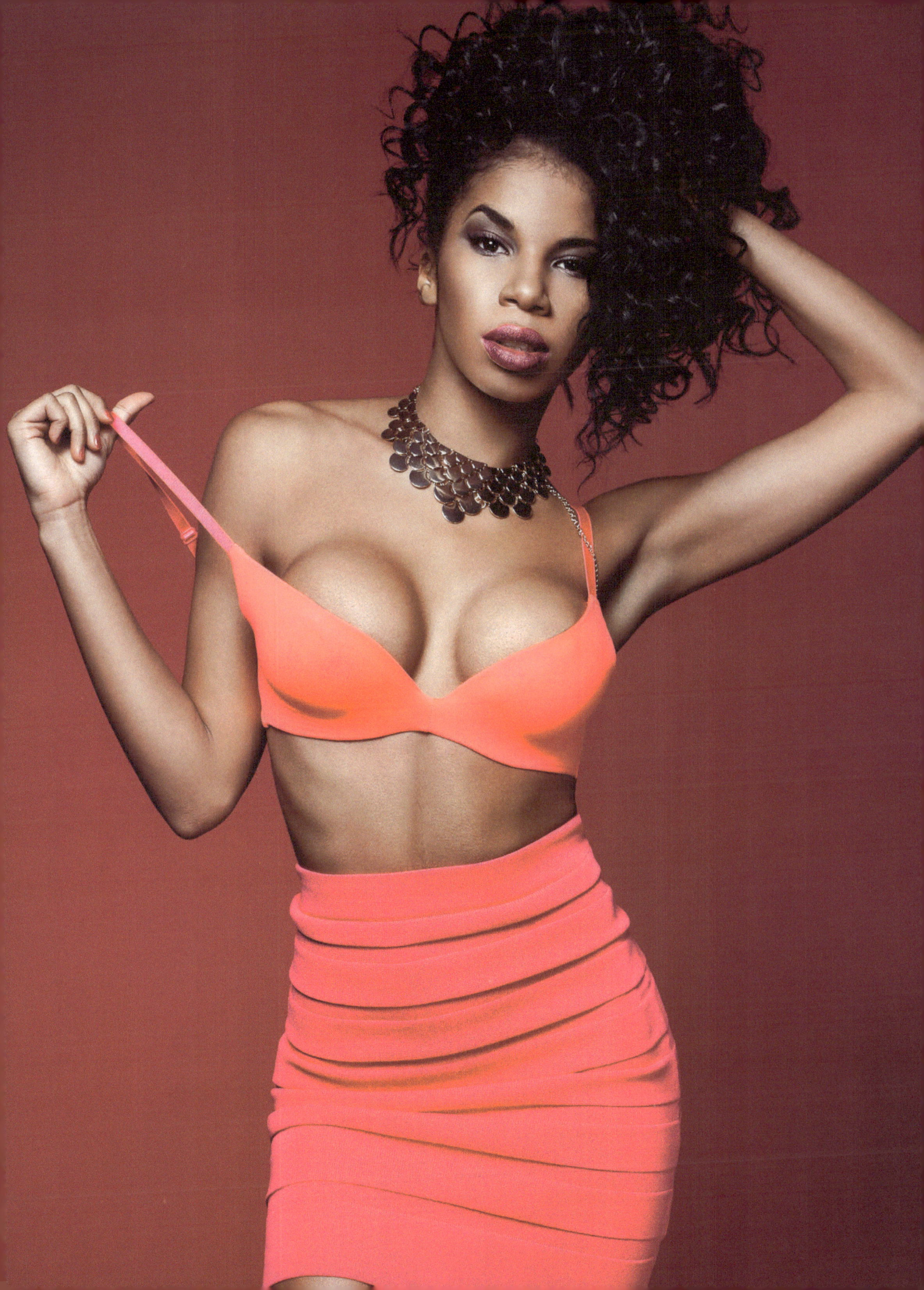

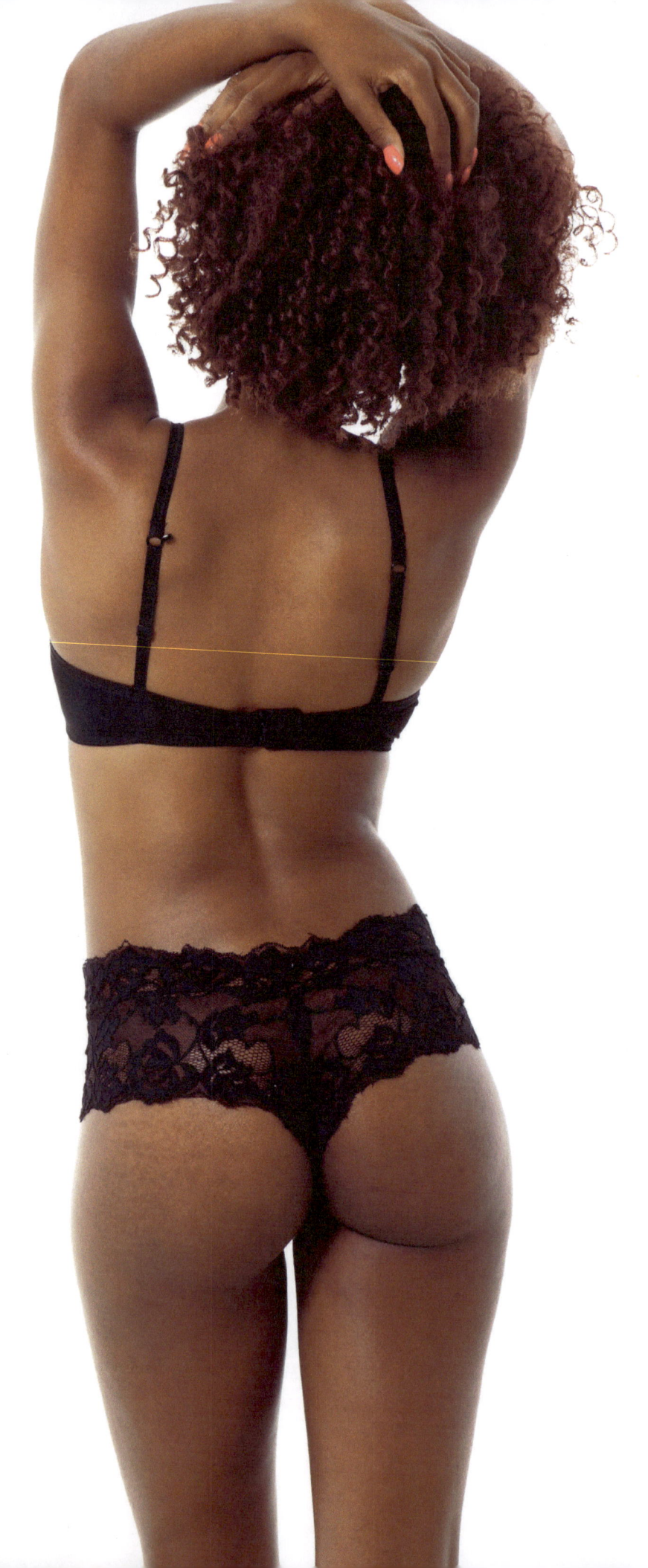

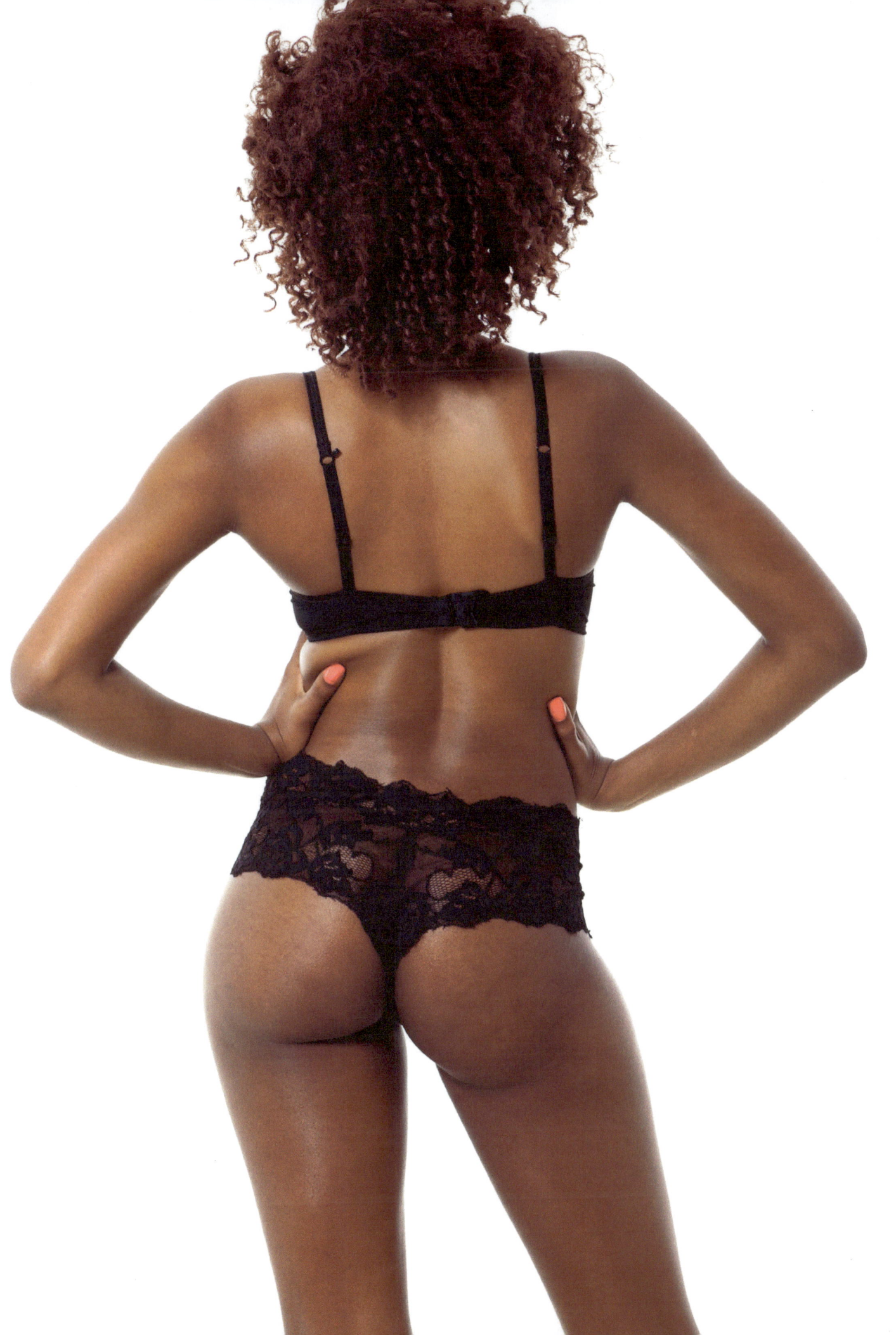

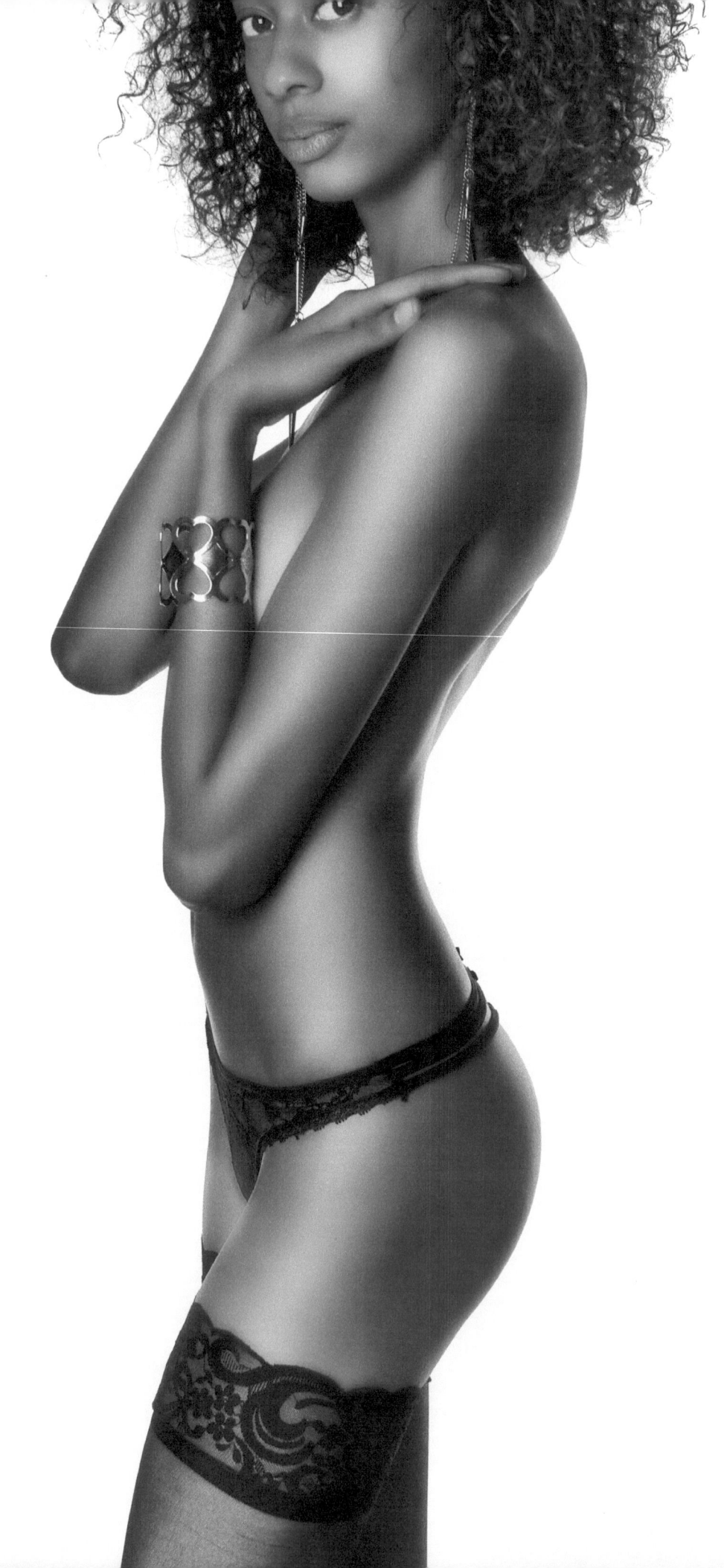

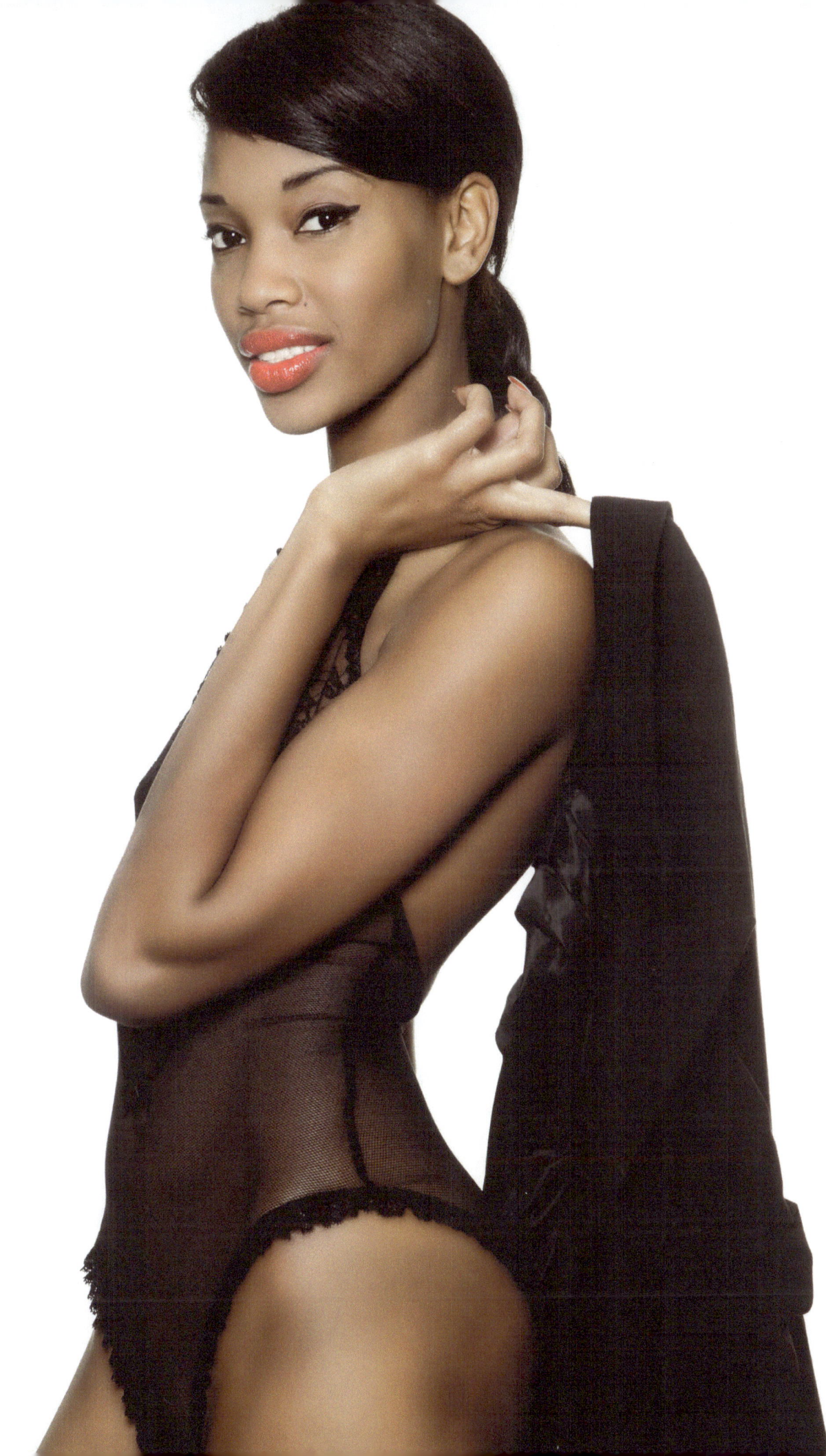

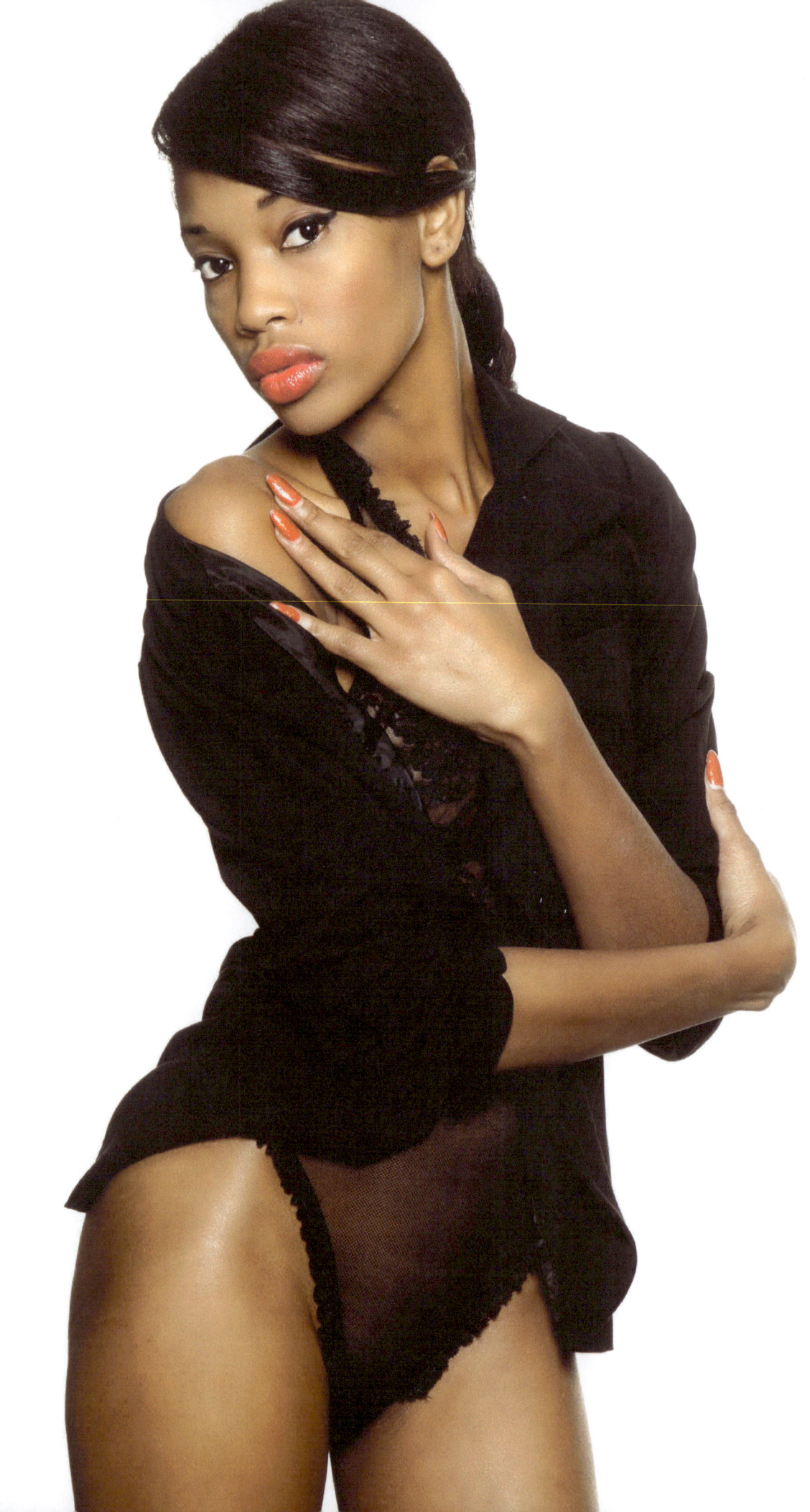

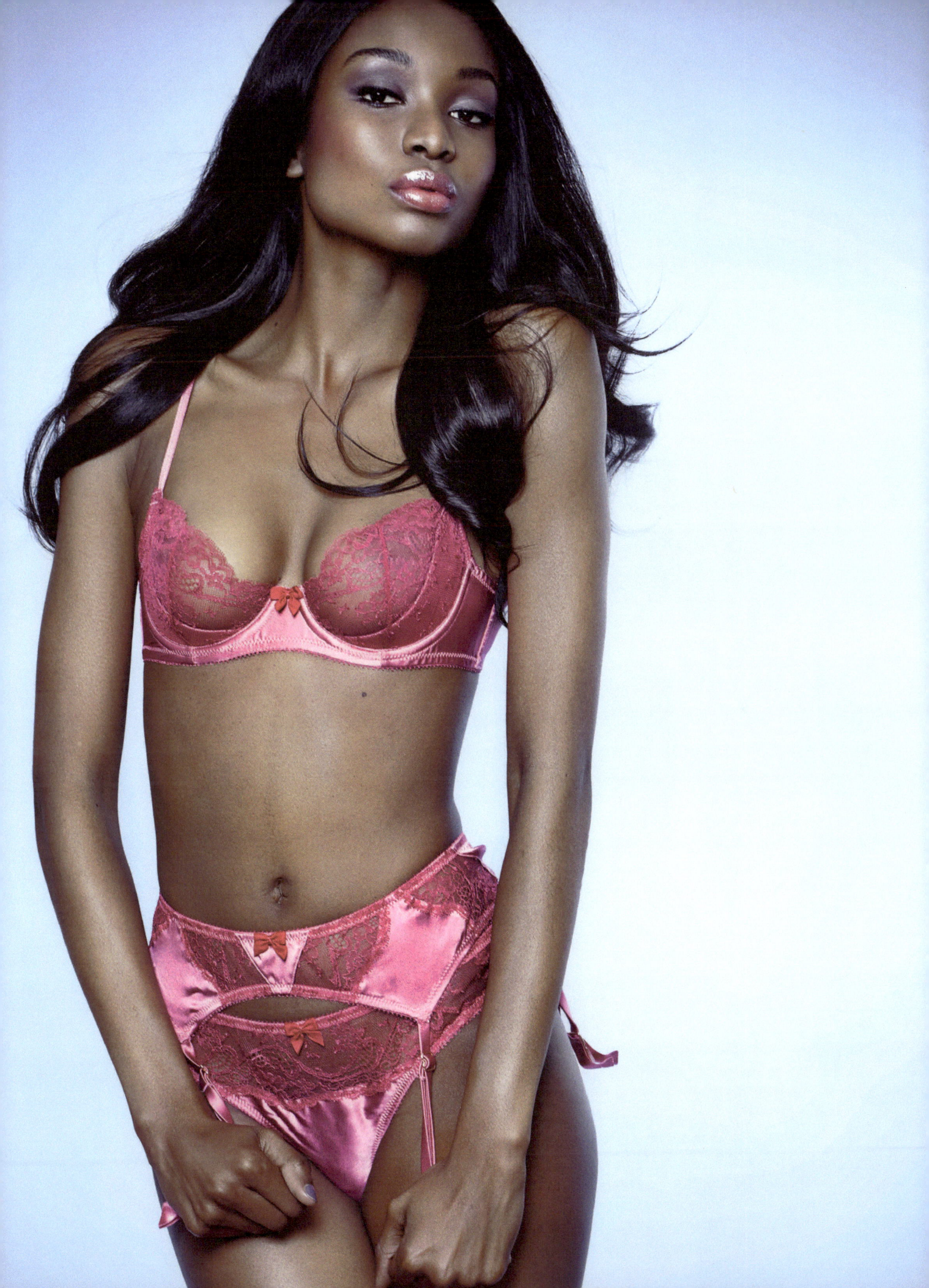

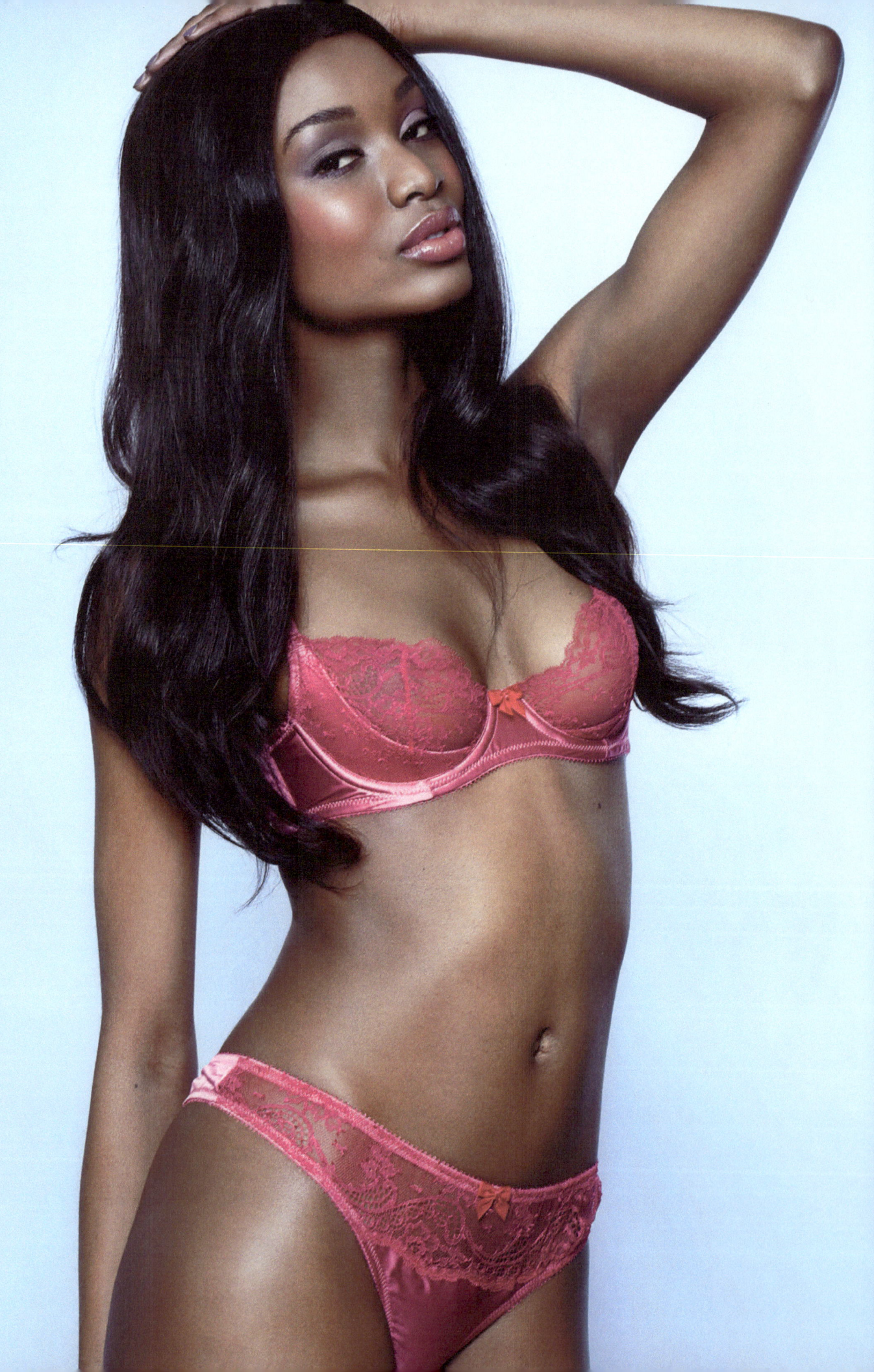

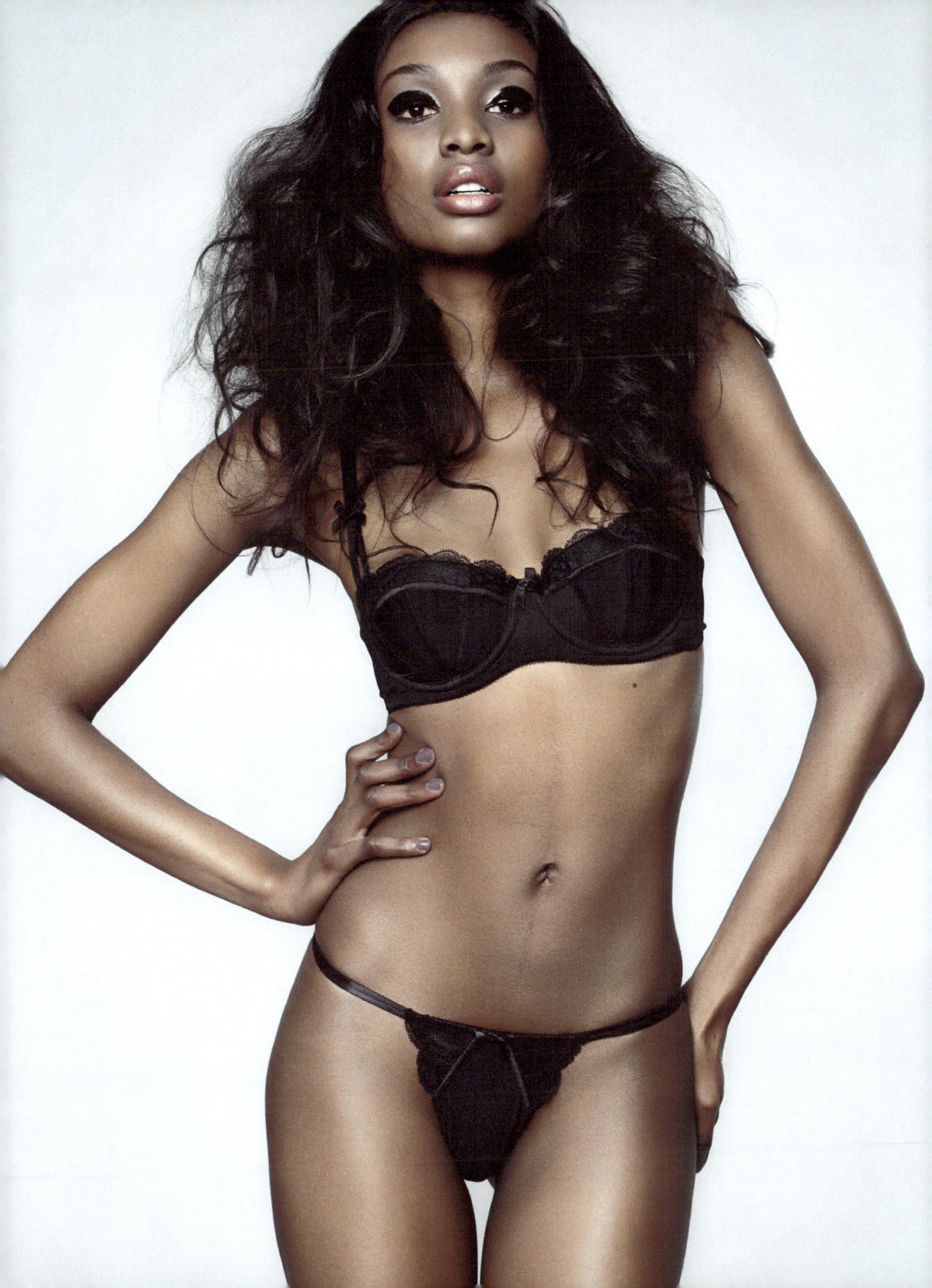

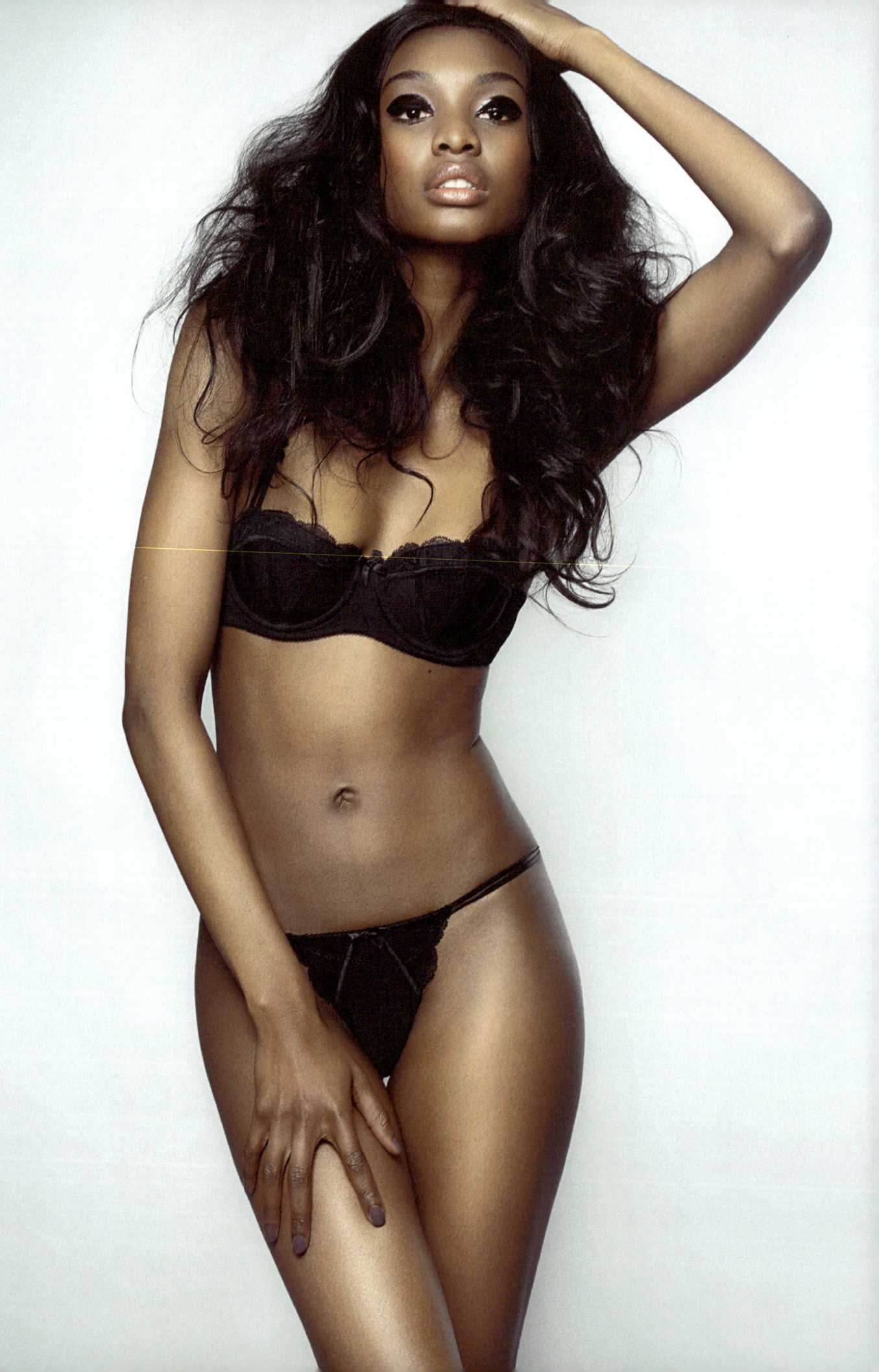

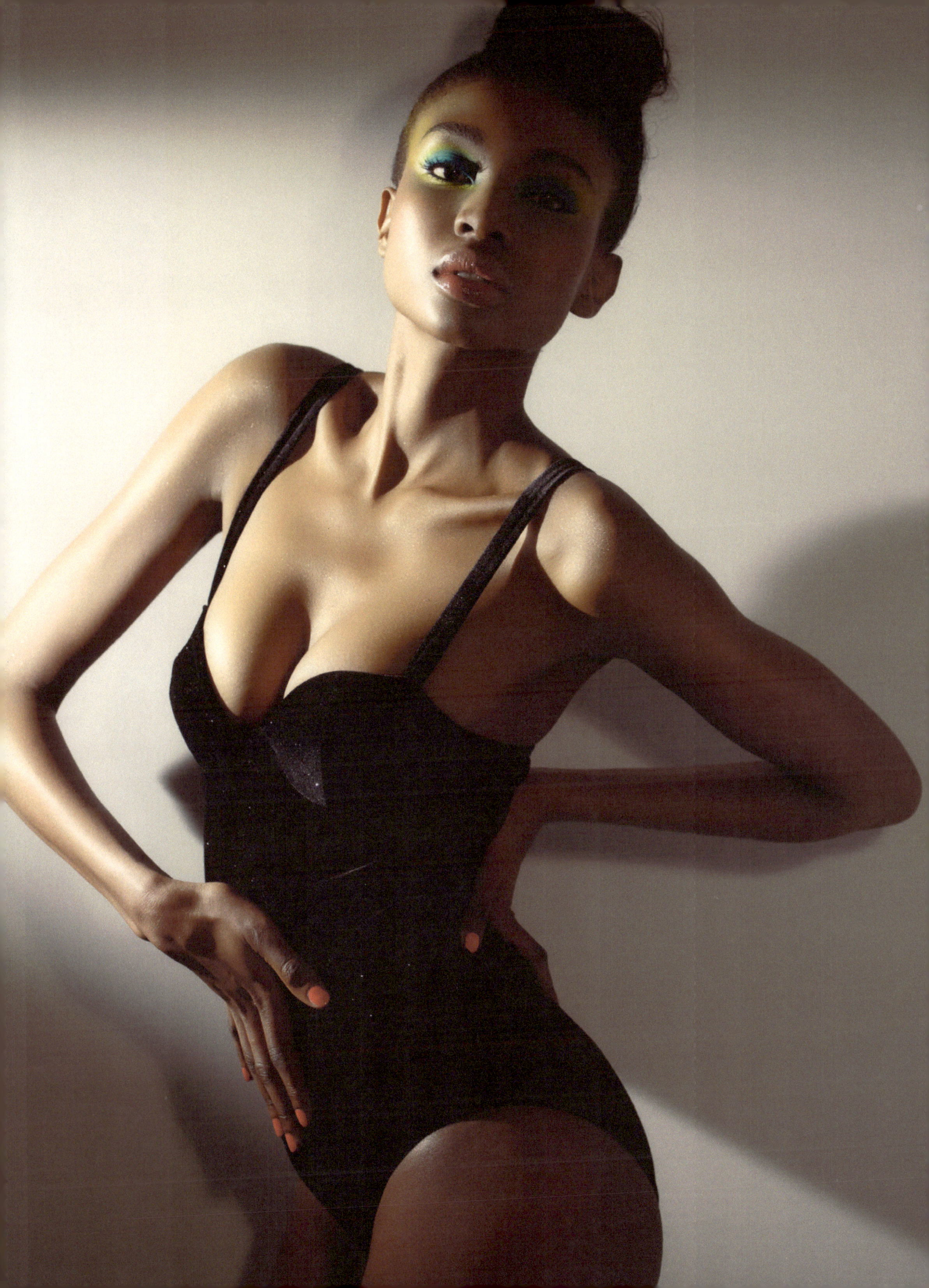

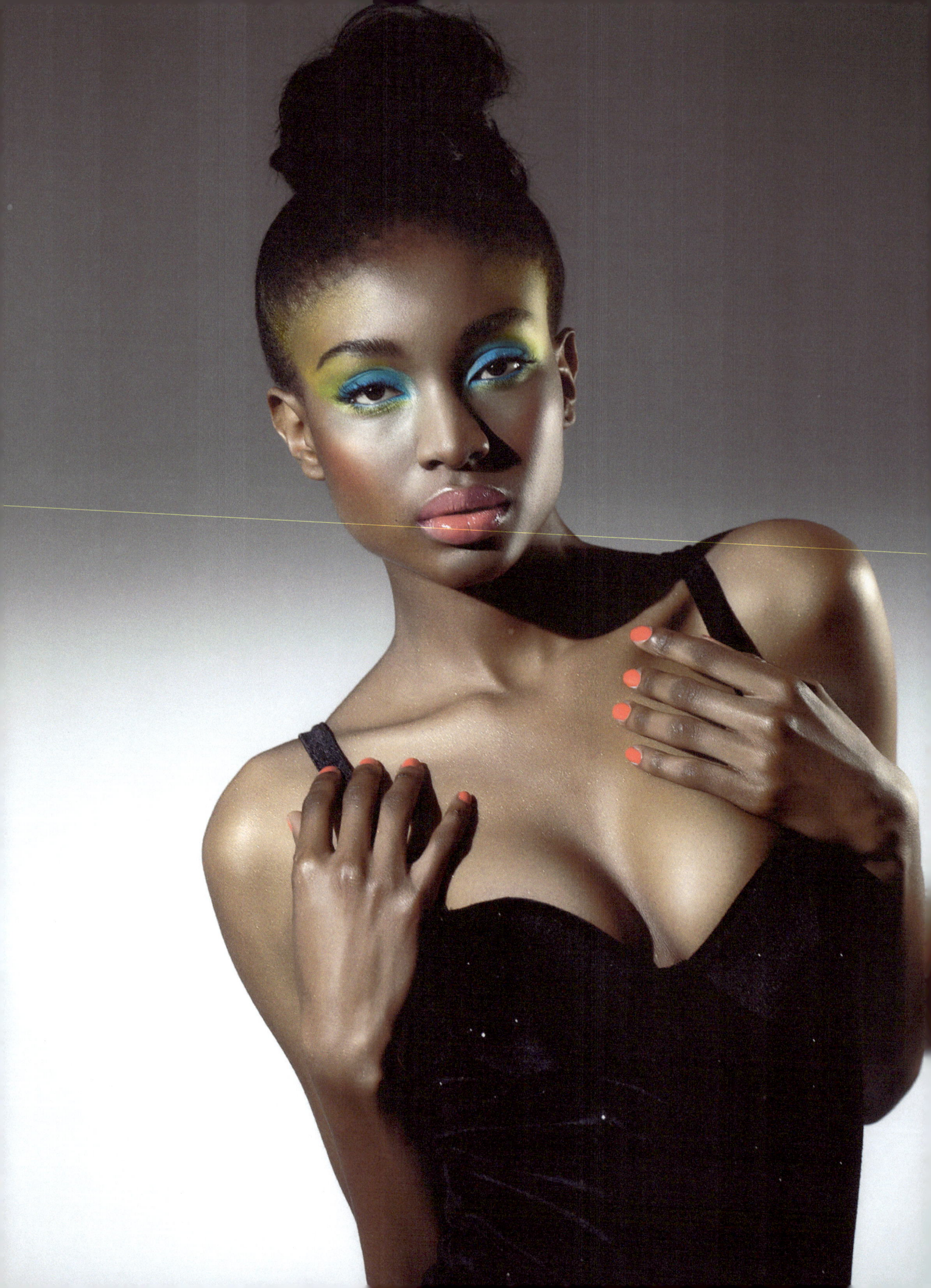

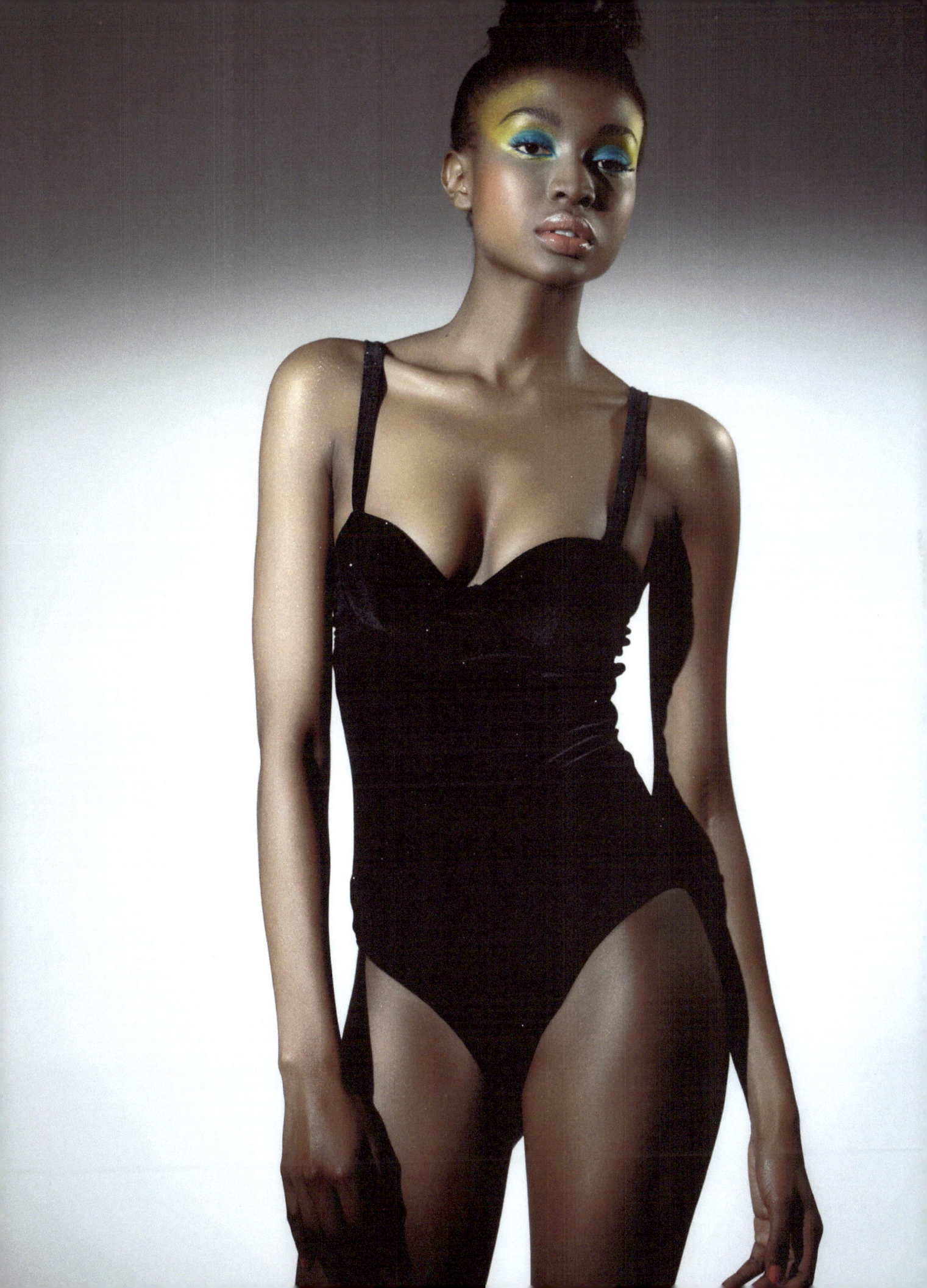